LIVING LIFE GOD'S WAY

"HOW TO FOLLOW GOD'S BLUE-PRINT FOR MANKIND"
VOLUME ONE

LIVING LIFE GOD'S WAY

"HOW TO FOLLOW GOD'S BLUEPRINT FOR MANKIND"
VOLUME ONE

BY

DR. NORMAN E. HUTCHINS, SR.

Copyright ©2021 by Dr. Norman E. Hutchins, Sr. All rights reserved.

This book or any portion thereof may not be reproduced or used in any manner whatsoever without the express written permission of the publisher except for the use of brief quotations in a book review.

Unless otherwise indicated, all Scripture quotations are taken from the King James Version of the Bible.

Printed in the United States of America

Cover Design: Nicole Kinloch, Kreative Asset Management

Editor: LPW Editing & Consulting Services

First Edition, 2018

ISBN-13: 978-0578862880

ISBN-10: 0578862880

ISBN 978-0-578-86289-7 (e-book)

DEDICATION

First, I would like to dedicate this work to the giants of the faith who have impacted my life in so many ways, and have had very important roles in my spiritual growth and development. Chief among them are the Presiding Bishop of the Church of God in Christ, Bishop Charles E. Blake; the late Bishop G.E. Patterson; and the late Bishop Benjamin Crouch. Also, to my wife who is the love of my life, Lady Karen Hutchins. Last but not least, to my college professors, as well as the Dean of the Ministerial Training Theological Institute, Bishop Johnnie J. Young, my church family, and all of my associates across the country. Thank you for the encouragement to pen this work.

CONTENTS

FOREWORD ··1

PREFACE ··5

Chapter 1
THE FIRST FOUR COMMANDS TO MANKIND ········9

Chapter 2
ONE OF YOUR GREATEST ENEMIES...TIME ············31

Chapter 3
LIVING IN THE "GLORY LANE" ···························· 47

Chapter 4
BREAKING THE SPIRIT OF RELIGION ···················59

Chapter 5
DEVELOPING FIVE SPIRITUAL HABITS ················· 73

Chapter 6
TRUSTING GOD THROUGH DIFFICULT TIMES ······91

Chapter 7
MY JOSEPH STORY ··103

FOREWORD

Living Life God's Way by Norman E. Hutchins is one of those books that is hard to put down once you've gotten it into your hands. It's listed among the few books that are the most interesting reads for me. Living Life God's Way will certainly not disappoint and will cause great encouragement and excitement, especially in times of bewilderment and uncertainty in the game of life. This well-written book specifically helps those who are enduring difficult times and struggling with the call to do the will and work of God.

Bishop Hutchins addresses real issues that plague many of us who are faced with a multitude of challenges as we maneuver through the maze of our Christian walk and press toward the mark of the high calling in Christ Jesus.

Bishop Hutchins once preached a sermon entitled "Trusting God Through Difficult Times." In this book, he shows how this specific message was designed to help those who have or are currently considering the cost of doing ministry, and the resulting effects on their personal lives and the lives of their families.

If you are suffering from challenges and obstacles

Foreword

which arise from doing the work of ministry, this book will offer a pathway to start living in the "Glory Lane," which is a defined track or path and a particular way of life for Believers. Glory represents the manifested presence of Almighty God showing up in our lives, and becoming whatever we need Him to be.

Bishop Hutchins has uniquely penned this book, providing a blueprint for understanding the heart and mind of God. Living Life God's Way is easy to understand and communicates Biblical truths that offer guidance and inspiration.

Bishop Hutchins' command of the English language and his unique conversational tone allow Biblical truths to become more memorable and meaningful. Living Life God's Way has been carefully designed to guide readers directly into the presence of God, where a God-desired consciousness and mindset are certain to leave a lasting, and indelible impression.

In today's self-centered society, Bishop Hutchins illustrates the importance of living life based on Biblical principles without being offensive. After reading Living Life God's Way, and meditating on it, you are sure to feel a renewed sense of empowerment to live a selfless lifestyle. Helpful personal anecdotes and Bible stories illustrate the importance of depending on God rather than on the material things of this world.

The spiritual habits listed in this book are the ingredients needed for spiritual fitness. As Believers, we must be equipped for unexpected attacks from the enemy. If you haven't developed these spiritual habits, then I urge you to start now.

In conclusion, Living Life God's Way challenges and demands, informs and inspires. I encourage you to read it and be transformed. I believe this book will make you a better person. Personally, I am better for having read it and even more motivated in my quest for God's ever-loving grace and mercy.

~The Right Reverend Liston Page II, M.Div., S.T.M., Author of How to Survive Your Storm

PREFACE

With so many different religions and ideologies, sometimes it can be difficult to understand which path to follow. Being exposed to culture, customs, man-made religious rituals, false doctrines, denominational expectations, and religious patterns, carved by the lack of understanding and the revelation of God's Word can make it difficult for the average believer who is only seeking to follow God (and not man's) religious traditions.

I was inspired to pen this book to help anyone who has a hunger and thirst for a relationship with God that does not require any method other than salvation and obedience to God's Word. If you are being taught that the only way you can have a proper relationship with God is through man-made doctrines, customs and religious requirements, but all you want is God, then this book is for you.

God did not create religion. It was created as man's attempt to correct his own unrighteousness; that's why Adam sewed fig leaves together. So, any attempt to clothe ourselves apart from the righteousness of God is religion, and any requirement deemed essential for personal salvation that is not endorsed by the revelation of

Preface

God's Word is religion.

Living life God's way is to understand God's blueprint for mankind through the heart and mind of God Himself. When we interpret God, we have to be careful not to put our own twist on it to fit our own propensities, but rather seek to understand God's law from the One who gave it.

"With all thy getting, get understanding…"
(Proverbs 4:7b)

~Dr. Norman E Hutchins, Sr.

CHAPTER 1
"THE FIRST FOUR COMMANDS TO MANKIND"

²⁷ So God created man in his own image, in the image of God created he him; male and female created he them.
²⁸ And God blessed them, and God said unto them, be fruitful, and multiply, and replenish the earth, and subdue it and to have dominion over the fish of the sea, and over the fowl of the air, and over every living thing that moveth upon the earth. -Genesis 1:27-28

After God created man, the first four commands He gave were to help govern man's life, and to help mankind experience the quality of life he was created for was:

Be fruitful, multiply, subdue, and have dominion.

These four commands are not optional, but are God's expectation for His creation. When we manifest these commands, it brings glory to our Creator. God never asks for a withdrawal where He has not made a deposit. The command to be fruitful comes from what God has deposited inside of us.

Our gifts and talents are part of His deposit in us, and when we cultivate our God-given gifts and talents, in the process of time they begin to produce fruit.

To be fruitful means to produce in abundance. One fruit seed produces an abundance of fruit, that's why God's command was to be fruitful. One of the lessons I've learned in ministry is that God only plants the seed. We must grow it, cultivate it and harvest it. Often, we want God to do everything but reap the harvest. But we must draw from everything that He has put inside of us to grow the seed. If the seed never produces fruit, it is never the fault of God, because not only did He plant the seed in us, He also gave us the capacity to grow it to harvest.

In the book of Matthew, Jesus taught a parable about talents. There are some valuable principles we should observe to help us better understand God's first command to be fruitful.

Matthew 25:14-18
¹⁴ For the kingdom of heaven is as a man traveling into a far country, who called his own servants, and delivered unto them his goods.
¹⁵ And unto one he gave five talents, to another two, and to another one; to every man according to his several ability; and straightway took his journey.
¹⁶ Then he that had received the five talents went and traded with the same, and made them other five talents.
¹⁷ And likewise he that had received two, he also gained other two.
¹⁸ But he that had received one went and digged in the earth, and hid his lord's money.

In this parable, the master gave his servants talents, which was money, but he never told them how to invest it. The master knew when he gave them the talents, that they had the capacity to make a profit. That's why the Scripture said, **"he gave to every man according to his several abilities."** That indicates that they were to use their gifts and talents to come up with an idea to generate a profit. The ability to do that was already in them.

When God gives us a seed, He already knows that we have the ability to be fruitful because He doesn't ask for what we are unable to do.

The servant who had one talent did not generate a profit. Not because he didn't have the ability, but because he failed to recognize that he had the wherewithal to increase, so, he buried it.

Why do people bury their gifts and talents and never produce fruit? Most of the time it is because they do not believe in their own abilities. Of course, when your seed, gifts and talents are introduced to an environment of fear, doubt, and unbelief, it becomes difficult for your seed to grow in that environment.

Your seed has to be planted in the soil of faith. When your seed is wrapped up in the soil of faith, you understand that it takes time for a seed to grow, and you also understand that the harvest does not come overnight.

In 1985, I was given a seed in the form of a song. I planted it and cultivated it. I remember singing it at every local church I could in my little hometown of Georgetown, DE. In 1991, seven years later, that same seed produced a harvest and now it can be heard around the world. It is entitled "God's Got A Blessing With My Name On It."

An oak tree doesn't grow overnight. It starts out as a seed. A fruit tree starts out as a seed. When God puts a gift, talent, dream, or vision inside of you, just like an oak tree, it starts as a seed.

Galatians 6:9
And let us not be weary in well doing: for in due season we shall reap, if we faint not.

If you prayed and asked God for an oak tree, He would give you an acorn, because the blessing of God usually comes in seed form. It becomes our responsibility to put the hard work behind it. The Bible says, "Faith without works is dead." Every cultivated seed has a harvest, but every seed needs the soil and the Word of God is the soil for your seed.

Joshua 1:8
This book of the law shall not depart out of thy mouth; but thou shalt meditate therein day and night, that thou mayest observe to do according to all that is written therein: for then thou shalt make thy way prosperous, and then thou shalt have good success.

The command of God for us to be fruitful comes from our commitment to the Word of God. And, because His Word is the living water we flourish in, no seed can grow outside of that water and soil. In the same way, no dream or vision can grow without the watering of God's Word.

Psalm 1:2-3
² But his delight is in the law of the Lord; and in his law doth he meditate day and night.
³ And he shall be like a tree planted by the rivers of water, that bringeth forth his fruit in his season; his leaf also shall not wither; and whatsoever he doeth shall prosper.

One of my favorite parables taught by Jesus in Matthew 13 is about The Sower. Jesus said that a sower went out to sow seeds, and some of the seeds fell by the wayside. Some of the seeds fell on stony places, some of the seeds fell among thorns, but other seeds fell on good ground and brought forth fruit.

The reason the seeds brought forth fruit is because they were planted in an environment that stimulated their growth. In this parable taught by Jesus, the good ground represents the Word of God; meaning when the Word of God is planted in your heart, it stimulates the growth of your seeds.

On the other hand, the reason the seeds that fell on all the other places mentioned could not grow, is because those seeds were in the wrong environments.

You cannot be fruitful if your seeds are not in the right environment. The Word of God produces a faith environment for your seeds, just as a natural seeds need an environment of soil, water and sunshine. Your spiritual seeds, which are your gifts and talents, need the environment of the Word of God to be your spiritual soil, water and sunshine.

When a farmer plants seeds, all he can do is plant them, cultivate them, pull weeds from around them, and watch them grow. He cannot make it rain, nor can he make the sun shine on his seeds. He faithfully plants his seeds, and prays for rainfall and sunshine.

When we do everything that we can with our spiritual seeds, God will send the rain and the sun, because the Word of God is our soil.

Here is the part of sowing seeds that really ministered to me. When seeds are planted in the soil, they start growing underground first, where it's dark, covered up, and all alone. Before you and I can be fruitful, our seeds also must start underground, where no one knows you, no one helps you, and no one recognizes the value of your seeds because they are covered. But when the seeds reach a certain age of maturity, they break through the soil where they can be seen.

Once they break through the soil, they are exposed to new elements, like rain, storms and wind. But the reason some plants survive these new elements, is because while the seeds were underground in a dark place, they were growing roots.

Plants survive in the new place because they grow roots in the dark place. The Bible talks about being rooted in God (Colossians 2:7), because before your gifts and talents come to fruition, you will face many different elements such as disappointment, discouragement, setbacks, betrayal and on and on.

You succeed because you're planted in the soil of the Word of God. You're not affected by the different elements because you started in a dark place and developed your roots. So, my question to you is, "Are you good ground?"

Another principle I have learned in ministry is that the death of a thing doesn't mean it is the end of a thing!

John 12:24
Verily, verily, I say unto you, Except a corn of wheat fall into the ground and die, it abideth alone: but if it die, it bringeth forth much fruit.

This teaches me that if I want my fruit to die, then I will live after the flesh. But, if I want my fruit to live, then I must mortify the deeds of my body (Romans 8:13). One of the definitions of the word mortify is to practice self-denial of one's body and appetites. The Scriptures call it "the works of the flesh."

Galatians 5:19-21
[19] Now the works of the flesh are manifest, which are these; Adultery, fornication, uncleanness, lasciviousness,
[20] Idolatry, witchcraft, hatred, variance, emulations, wrath, strife, seditions, heresies,
[21] Envyings, murders, drunkenness, revellings, and such like: of the which I tell you before, as I have also told you in time past, that they which do such things shall not inherit the kingdom of God.

A growing plant has to be protected from anything that has the possibility of killing it before harvest time. Likewise, our fruit, gifts and talents must be protected from the works of the flesh, to ensure that our fruit is not contaminated by the deeds of our body. The reason this is so important to God is because contaminated people contaminate people. When we first mortify our flesh, something in us has got to die.

A contaminated seed will only produce contaminated fruit. God will not take you where your character cannot keep you.

The reason it is hard to mortify your flesh, is because you cannot mortify your flesh through the flesh. That would be like telling sin not to sin, when all sin knows is to sin. The Scripture teaches that we must mortify our flesh through the Spirit, and for that to happen, our spirit man has got to be stronger than our fleshly man.

Our spirit man helps to activate our fruit, because God never speaks to our gifts or our talents; He speaks to our spirit and our spirit stimulates our gifts.

If we are not built up in faith, prayer, and in the Word of God, our flesh will fight against our spirit, and most of the time, it will win.

Always remember that your spirit and flesh are enemies.

Galatians 5:17
For the flesh lusteth against the Spirit, and the Spirit against the flesh: and these are contrary the one to the other: so that ye cannot do the things that ye would.

For example, we have a person in the right corner who runs every day, works out for hours each day, watches what he eats, spend hours looking at video footage, and gets plenty of rest. Meanwhile, the guy in the left corner, never runs, never exercises, has bad eating habits, stays up all night, and never studies the video footage of his opponent.

Who do you think will win? Of course, it's no question that the guy in the right corner has the advantage. When the spirit and flesh step into the ring, only the strong will survive.

The first commandment of the Bible for mankind to be fruitful was given before sin entered the picture. There was nothing to prevent man from being productive, but after sin was introduced to the world, we had an enemy whose primary concentration was to prevent the children of God from bearing fruit.

John 10:10
The thief cometh not, but for to steal, and to kill, and to destroy: I am come that they might have life, and that they might have it more abundantly.

The second command God gave to mankind was to multiply, and replenish the earth.

In the Basic English translation of the Bible, multiply means to "be fertile and have increase, and make the earth full." The Word of God's translation of multiply is "to increase in numbers." In The Good News translation, multiply means "to have many children so that your descendants will live all over the earth."

Notice that God gave Adam this command in the first chapter of Genesis, but Eve was not created until the second chapter. So, why would God command Adam to multiply before Eve was created? It's because God was calling out of the man what he put inside of him at creation.

After God created Adam, He never went back to the dirt. Adam multiplied and replenished the earth because God took the woman out of him. Then, Adam took the baby out of the woman; he took the family out of the children; and the children multiplied into nations; and now we have billions of people on planet earth. But it all started from one man.

One of the greatest miracles of mankind is that we are able to multiply and reproduce ourselves. I believe this command of God to multiply is not just limited to reproducing ourselves through children, but anything we touch or attempt to do should always multiply.

Psalm 1:3
And he shall be like a tree planted by the rivers of water, that bringeth forth his fruit in his season; his leaf also shall not wither; and whatsoever he doeth shall prosper.

Whatever he does shall prosper, speaks to increase, which is man's natural instinct. That instinctual part of God's nature was planted inside every man and woman at creation. That's why when we increase, we feel fulfilled, and when we decrease, we feel dissatisfied. Even little children have a natural instinct to increase. They are not satisfied with only counting to ten, they want to learn how to count to fifty, and then one hundred. If you lose your instinct to increase, life will come to a standstill.

Psalm 115:14
The LORD shall increase you more and more, you and your children.

To multiply is to increase. When God breathed into us the breath of life, the ability to increase was in His breath. When we tap into our God-given natural ability, being fruitful and multiplying becomes second nature to us. If our young children do not increase or multiply in learning, we become very concerned; as a matter of fact, we will take them to a specialist to get a diagnosis. But when we do not increase or multiply spiritually, we are not as concerned; however, this is not an option from God. It is natural for man to be fruitful and multiply.

The third and fourth command given to mankind at creation was to subdue and have

dominion.

We will discuss the two at the same time because they both work together. To subdue means to be in charge; one Bible translation says "rule over it," which means to have legal authority.
Dominion means domain or territory. God placed man in the garden to dress it and keep it. What does all this mean?

God placed man on planet Earth to be its manager. He was to rule and be the supreme authority over the domain and territory called earth. That means man would be responsible for his own success or failure. God even created a law for Himself that would prevent His illegal interference into mankind's affairs, when He said, "Let them have dominion." Therefore, the condition of our world is a result of mankind's mismanagement. Man's disobedience was a free will act that introduced sin into man's domain.

Romans 5:19
For as by one man's disobedience many were made sinners, so by the obedience of one shall many be made righteous.

When sin was introduced, man had two more options to manage, good and bad. Because, before the fall of man, God only gave him one "off limit" command.

Genesis 2:16-17
[16] And the LORD God commanded the man, saying, Of every tree of the garden thou mayest freely eat:
[17] But of the tree of the knowledge of good and evil, thou shalt not eat of it: for in the day that thou eatest thereof thou shalt surely die.

Man's sin nature brought with it a lustful desire for things that he wanted as opposed to things that he needed; and this challenged his ability to subdue and have dominion over his domain. This, in turn led to poor choices and bad management.

The reason Jesus came to the earth was because of man's mismanagement. The reason Jesus was God in the flesh is because the only way He would not be violating His own law of interference was to become a man. His assignment on earth was to reconcile man back to God so that the legal authority over earth that was given to Satan through the fall of man would be taken back from Satan and given to mankind, God's creation.

Ephesians 1:22-23
[22] And hath put all things under his feet, and gave him to be the head over all things to the church,
[23] Which is his body, the fulness of him that

> *filleth all in all.*
>
> *Matthew 16:19*
> *And I will give unto thee the keys of the kingdom of heaven: and whatsoever thou shalt bind on earth shall be bound in heaven: and whatsoever thou shalt loose on earth shall be loosed in heaven.*

Thus, we have legal authority over the earth and everything in it. But the only way we can now activate that authority is through salvation and obedience to God.

Illegitimate authority is what Satan exhibited when he rebelled against the law of God. As a result, He lost the authority that he had, and like Satan, when we rebelled against the law of God, we too lost our authority to subdue and have dominion.

Earlier, I mentioned that God created a law allowing Himself to interfere in man's affairs on earth, and that law is called "prayer."

> *Philippians 4:6*
> *Be careful for nothing; but in every thing by prayer and supplication with thanksgiving let your requests be made known unto God.*

Prayer is the legal license for God to interfere.

So, when we are facing something we cannot subdue, prayer gives God permission to interfere. Now, I know the thought that just crossed your mind. You are thinking, "Well, I pray and pray, but I get no results."

One of the most important principles of prayer is you must pray under legal authority. This means that when you accept Jesus Christ as your Savior, according to Romans 10:9, and walk in obedience to His laws, God recognizes your legal authority. Practicing sin will always prevent God from intervening.

1 Peter 3:12
For the eyes of the Lord are over the righteous, and his ears are open unto their prayers: but the face of the Lord is against them that do evil.

When you have not submitted yourself to the law of God, He recognizes that as rebellion, which is illegitimate authority. Another principle of prayer is that it gives God permission to interfere, but faith gets the job done.

Hebrews 11:6
But without faith it is impossible to please him: for he that cometh to God must believe that he is, and that he is a rewarder of them that diligently seek him.

Faith is knowing the facts, yet trusting God's Word. In 2005, because of complications of diabetes, I became blind. I was the pastor of a church that my wife and I birthed only four years prior. I was devastated, because usually when you go blind from diabetes, it is irreversible.

I went through four surgeries with no success, and the facts were that I was blind, and my chances of seeing again were uncertain. I was facing a situation that would test my authority and would determine if I had the ability to subdue and have dominion. Well, I knew the facts, but I chose to believe what God said.

Isaiah 53:5
But he was wounded for our transgressions, he was bruised for our iniquities: the chastisement of our peace was upon him; and with his stripes we are healed.

I know the Scripture says "now faith is the substance of things hoped for," but what I've learned is that faith does not always produce same day results. My faith had to become the sustainer of my hope until the manifestation of the miracle came. Instead of having a pity party, I stepped up my game. I preached every Sunday, taught Bible Study on Tuesday nights, worked in the administrative office Monday through Friday, did counseling, and handled just about all of my pastoral duties, while at the same time knowing the facts, but believing what God said.

I preached faith to my faith, and then one night in prayer, I made a statement to God that I believe sealed my miracle. I said to Him, "Lord, I believe that You are going to give me my sight back, but if I never see again, I will continue to love You and serve You with all my heart."

After six months of being blind, one Sunday morning I was preaching from the subject, "This Is Not How My Story Ends!" I remember the power of God was so heavy in that place, and at the end of my sermon, the Holy Spirit spoke to me and said, "Because of your faithfulness, and the assignment God has for your life, today will be the last day anyone leads you through the church."

Six days later, on a Saturday night, I went to sleep blind, but when I woke up that Sunday morning, for the first time in a very long time, I saw my wife's face! I even had enough vision to walk through the church on my own. Praise God!

When you walk in authority by obeying God's Word and totally submitting yourself to God, your prayer will be answered, because it is your legal authority. So, the command to be fruitful, multiply, subdue and have dominion is the authority given to mankind from God to assist us in dominating our domain.

Just one act of unforgiving sin does not obligate God to intervene. David said, *"I have been young, and now am old; yet have I not seen the righteous forsaken, nor his seed begging bread." Psalm 37:25*

You and I are the righteousness of God, and begging is against His law.

Let me give you this last principle before we close this chapter. Because we are saved it does not exempt us from trouble. The Bible says it rains on the just as well as the unjust, but I like to put it like this, for the righteous and the faithful, it's a different kind of rain!

CHAPTER 2
ONE OF YOUR GREATEST ENEMIES...TIME

[1] And it came to pass after these things, that God did tempt Abraham, and said unto him, Abraham: and he said, Behold, here I am. [2] And he said, Take now thy son, thine only son Isaac, whom thou lovest, and get thee into the land of Moriah; and offer him there for a burnt offering upon one of the mountains which I will tell thee of. [3] And Abraham rose up early in the morning, and saddled his ass, and took two of his young men with him, and Isaac his son, and clave the wood for the burnt offering, and rose up, and went unto the place of which God had told him. [4] Then on the third day Abraham lifted up his eyes, and saw the place afar off.
-Genesis 22:1-4

The Scripture says that God tempted Abraham. To tempt means to test. It is not unusual for someone in the kingdom who is preparing for the next level of manifestation to be tested.

It is important to God that you possess the right character that goes along with promotion. Therefore, He takes us through seasons of testing to prove our character. A student of the Bible may ask, 'Isn't testing contradictory to the book of James?' James 1:13 says, "Let no man say when he is tempted, I am tempted of God: *for God cannot be tempted with evil, neither tempteth he any man."*

The understanding is found in the word tempt. While both God and Satan tempt man, God tempts man to perfect him, while Satan tempts man to pervert him.

God will never test man by tempting him to sin. God's testing is always designed to perfect character. Abraham was tested because of what God wanted to release in his life. Testing always comes before promotion.

Abram's first test can be seen in his name. Abram, means *exalted father*, but he had no son. Then, God changed his name to Abraham, which means *father of multitudes*, and he still had no son. Sometimes God will give you the name before He gives you what goes with it, and the test is by faith.

Can you walk in the name when you haven't gotten the manifestation? One of the lessons Abraham had to learn was what not to do while waiting on the promise. The mistake we often make is trying to help God out when things are not moving as fast as we would like.

The promise was Isaac, but Abraham's wife gave him her handmaiden to birth a child in place of the promise. In their attempt to help God out, they birthed Ishmael, but Isaac was the promise.

The question is, what do you do when the promise shows up, but you have created a problem? Now, you have a problem and a promise?

The principle is, *do not create a problem while you're waiting for the promise.*

Like Abraham, if you have a word from God that your Isaac is coming, the only thing to do is wait. As Christians, we often become impatient and begin to entertain other options. Satan often uses time to his advantage. He reasons that if given enough time with no manifestation of our promises, we will give up. But I encourage you my brother and sister, your greatest test is not the test of Satan, but it is the test of time.

Isaiah 40:31
But they that wait upon the Lord shall renew their strength; they shall mount up with wings as eagles; they shall run, and not be weary; and they shall walk, and not faint.

Each new dimension in God presents new tests. The bigger the blessing, the bigger and harder the test. Abraham's next test would prove to be any parent's worst nightmare.

Genesis 22:2
And he said, Take now thy son, thine only son Isaac, whom thou lovest, and get thee into the land of Moriah; and offer him there for a burnt offering upon one of the mountains which I will tell thee of.

To hear God say "sacrifice your son to Me as a burnt offering" has got to be one of the greatest tests anyone could face. Yet, with an obedient heart, Abraham was willing to do it. In the book of Hebrews, he is counted as righteous, but we also see his faith when he says we will return. After hearing God's request, how could Abraham still trust God?

Genesis 22:4-5
⁴ Then on the third day Abraham lifted up his eyes, and saw the place afar off.
⁵ And Abraham said unto his young men, Abide ye here with the ass; and I and the lad will go yonder and worship, and come again to you,

Abraham placed Isaac on the altar and was prepared to sacrifice him. It was only at the point of no return that God stepped in and stopped him.

So, what was this test all about? Are you willing to give up what you love the most to receive the manifestations of the promises God has for you? The blessing God had for Abraham was bigger than one son. And, because of his obedience, not only did he pass the test, but Isaac lived.

God wants to know if He is first in our lives. Is there anything we possess that He cannot have, even though He provided it?

Another principle that we must learn is that God has a set time for manifestation.

Galatians 6:9
And let us not be weary in well doing: for in due season we shall reap, if we faint not.

Your test comes to prepare you for your "due

season," so that when it comes, you will be well prepared to receive it with joy and thanksgiving; and you will have grown to the level of your blessing, so that your faithfulness to God will not be compromised.

God will sometimes use circumstances in our lives as tests.

I come from a large family. My mother had 12 children. Six boys and six girls, and I'm the baby boy. I started preaching at the age of eight and by the time I was 15 years old, I was traveling with my mother to North Carolina. There, I would preach at a church, not knowing that the pastor was my biological father. After he disowned me, I felt totally confused. A few years later, he died and I never had the opportunity to get to know him because he did not want his church to know that he had a son outside of his marriage.

Needless to say, I was bitter and harbored unforgiveness against him. It was a tragic situation that could happen to anyone, but God saw it as a test. Could I forgive him for disowning me? Or, would I continue to live the rest of my life as a prisoner to unforgiveness?

I remember standing at his graveside with tears in my eyes. I released him and forgave him even though he was dead. I now know that it wasn't as important for him to hear me as it was for me to release him. When I did, even though the situation was caused by bad choices that he made, I passed the test and moved on with my life to receive future blessings. God placed other powerful, influential men in my life to father me, teach me and help train me to be the man that I am today. One in particular is Bishop Charles E. Blake, the pastor of West Angeles Church of God in Christ in Los Angeles, CA. What my biological father wasn't to me, he was.

After Abraham passed his test, he went on to become a father of many nations and today, the earth is filled with his descendants. If you know anyone that you have not forgiven, that's your test and it is time to forgive.

Matthew 6:14-15
¹⁴ For if ye forgive men their trespasses, your heavenly Father will also forgive you:
¹⁵ But if ye forgive not men their trespasses, neither will your Father forgive your trespasses.

When you forgive, you break the chains of bondage, and free yourself to live a life of abundance. There are so many blessings waiting for you on the other side of forgiveness.

One of the ways you can tell if you have

genuinely forgiven someone is when you touch the wound but feel no pain. Your challenges in life can become your greatest tests, but when you face them with obedience to God and a heart of forgiveness, you will always come out on the winning side.

Exodus 3:1-4
¹ Now Moses kept the flock of Jethro his father in law, the priest of Midian: and he led the flock to the backside of the desert, and came to the mountain of God, even to Horeb.
² And the angel of the Lord appeared unto him in a flame of fire out of the midst of a bush: and he looked, and, behold, the bush burned with fire, and the bush was not consumed.
³ And Moses said, I will now turn aside, and see this great sight, why the bush is not burnt.
⁴ And when the Lord saw that he turned aside to see, God called unto him out of the midst of the bush, and said, Moses, Moses. And he said, Here am I.

A close look at the life of Moses reveals to us how time plays a very important factor in our spiritual growth and development, and prepares us for God's assignment for our lives.

Moses was born at a time when a decree was given to assassinate all male Hebrew babies. However, when the anointing is on your life, the enemy cannot destroy you.

Moses' mother hid him for three months. Then she placed him in a basket and set him afloat on the Nile River. One of the principles I learned there is that God can hide you for a season. I call it the test of time!

What do you do when you see other people doing what you know you have been anointed to do, and yet, at every turn it seems like the enemy is coming after you?

God's plan for Moses was to train him for his destiny in the very house that decreed his death. Now I know what David meant in Psalm 23:5, "Thou preparest a table before me in the presence of mine enemies."

Moses was discovered by the Pharaoh's daughter, and Moses' own mother was secured as his nurse. He was raised among the Egyptians in the palace, where he learned important leadership skills that would be helpful to him later in his journey. Another very important lesson to learn is to never despise where God has you in one season of your life. Become a student of it and learn all you can, because that season will come to an end. If you have not yet learned the lessons of the season, you may have to repeat it.

You only graduate to the next grade when you pass the test of the one you're in. After 40 years, Moses fled Egypt because he saw an Egyptian beating a Hebrew slave, which brings me to this point. It takes time to discover what's really inside of you that needs to be worked out.

Moses was now a murderer, but still called of God. He spent the next 40 years of his life in Midian, which was called the backside of the desert. It was there that he learned the skills of being a shepherd. This would later prove to be invaluable, as he would be leading God's sheep through the wilderness. In the last 40 years of his life, he went before Pharaoh with the experience of his past, but spoke the command of God, to let God's people go.

What can we learn from the life of Moses? The first 40 years of his life were spent in Egypt. The second 40 years of his life were spent in Midian, and the third 40 years of his life were spent in the wilderness. Moses lived to be 120 years old, and God used the first 80 years of his life to prepare him for the last 40. That is to say, his preparation was much longer than his performance!

Your preparation backstage takes much longer than your performance on stage. Anytime you see a play production on stage, the applause of the audience is not just for the night's performance, but for the many hours, weeks, and months of practice. That's where you may be right now. God has you backstage preparing you for your life's performance, so don't use this time to complain or doubt Him. Just get ready for your debut. Everything that Moses learned backstage would now challenge him in the wilderness. Moses' greatest challenge would be to lead two million people into their future, which was the land of promise, when they kept longing for the past of bondage, suffering and pain.

Exodus 14:11-12
[11] And they said unto Moses, Because there were no graves in Egypt, hast thou taken us away to die in the wilderness? wherefore hast thou dealt thus with us, to carry us forth out of Egypt?
[12] Is not this the word that we did tell thee in Egypt, saying, Let us alone, that we may serve the Egyptians? For it had been better for us to serve the Egyptians, than that we should die in the wilderness.

Moses had enough history with God to know that no matter what he and the Israelites faced in the wilderness, God would provide and protect them. That is one of the things that tests and time will do for you. It will give you a history with God, and it is the history of your past that gives you the courage to face your future.

When they had no water, God turned a rock into a faucet. When they had no food, God made it rain down manna, and when their enemies came to overtake them, God parted the waters of the Red Sea as the glory cloud led them by day and night.

This teaches me that the challenges of your future are diminished by the victories of your past. God made them a promise that He would lead them into the land of Canaan. So, no matter what you face on your journey, it cannot destroy you, because you have an expected end.

Jeremiah 29:11
For I know the thoughts that I think toward you, saith the Lord, thoughts of peace, and not of evil, to give you an expected end.

Those who started out for Canaan were not the ones who eventually ended up in Canaan. The reason for this is, they started out believing in the promise, but through the test of time their faith wavered, which led them to complain. Complaining is contrary to faith in God, and signifies a lack of trust in God's Word. Complaining magnifies your problem, and many times changes the course of action God wanted to take in blessing you.

Numbers 14:27-29
²⁷ How long shall I bear with this evil congregation, which murmur against me? I have heard the murmurings of the children of Israel, which they murmur against me.
²⁸ Say unto them, As truly as I live, saith the Lord, as ye have spoken in mine ears, so will I do to you:
²⁹ Your carcasses shall fall in this wilderness; and all that were numbered of you, according to your whole number, from twenty years old and upward, which have murmured against me,

It's not a sin to be concerned, but it is a sin to complain. The Bible teaches us to speak those things that are not as though they were. One of the lessons I've learned is if I cannot confess anything good about my circumstances, then I say nothing at all, because the Bible says you have what you say, and your words have power.

Proverbs 18:21
Death and life are in the power of the tongue: and they that love it shall eat the fruit thereof.

When the Scripture mentions the power of the tongue, the word tongue is translated "speech or language." The words that come out of your mouth have the power of life or death to our future. The bigger picture is this, when God hears you speak powerful words, even though presently you may be in a dark place, it pleases Him, and a breakthrough is closer than you think.

So, as I close this chapter, and I better close, because I feel the anointing, let me encourage you! You never get a harvest until something is planted, so plant your faith, and when the season is right, you will produce a harvest, but you must pass the test of time.

CHAPTER 3
Living In the "Glory Lane"

For I reckon that the sufferings of this present time are not worthy to be compared with the glory which shall be revealed in us. -Romans 8:18

Living in the "Glory Lane" has to do with walking a well-defined track or path; which is a way of life for the believers. We were created for this. The glory represents the manifested presence of almighty God showing up in your life, and becoming whatever you need Him to be.

If you need healing, it's in the glory. If you need peace, it's in the glory. Whatever you need, it's in the glory. I have been preaching now for forty-eight years. I was called to preach when I was just eight years old.

I remember living in a small town called Millsboro, DE, and my grandfather was a sharecropper who farmed chickens. I remember helping him collect the eggs. And boy, you have never seen so many eggs! We had about fifty thousand chickens to take care of and raise for a poultry plant.

When I was eight years old, I would preach to the chickens. I would repeat the sermon I heard the pastor preach and I would tell the chickens, "You need to be saved!" Later that year, we were at church and the youth did a service one Sunday afternoon. I was asked to give a sermonette, and the power of God was on me so strong, that my pastor and my mother could tell that the hand of God was on my life. I was known then as the traveling eight-year-old evangelist.

By the time I turned twelve, I was ordained as a minster and my mother had me preaching up and down the East Coast. I would preach at night, then go to school the very next day.

At 19, I was ordained as an Elder in the church and then pastored my first church, New Hope Church of God in Christ at the age of 20. I moved to California at age 25 to continue my studies, but several years later, I returned home and

Living In The "Glory Lane"

birthed Frontline Ministries. That's when the enemy started throwing every attack he could throw at me.

My health was attacked like never before. But when you are living in the Glory Lane, you may go through some stuff, but it will always produce glory. No one gets a mountaintop blessing without a valley experience. In this chapter, I want to share with you some of my valley experiences so you can better understand my mountaintop blessings. This testimony will be faith for your valley!

In July of 2014, Mr. Kris Patrick, Founder and Publisher of *PATH MEGAzine* exclusively interviewed my lovely wife, Karen and I. Here's the article in its entirety:

> *"As distinguishable as someone's name can be to large audiences, we often find that real struggle is a lonely battle. With so much bad news going on in society today, it's good to hear a story of restoration and faith impact the Gospel community.*
>
> *Gospel music legend, Bishop Norman Hutchins recently shared his testimony with PATH MEGAzine. An interview that left Hutchins in tears as he recalled the horror that his family felt when seeing him with no*

pulse on the rigid confines of a hospital bed. Just 8 months ago, the Pastor of Frontline Ministries in Dover, Delaware was promoting his new album 'Hosanna', when a doctor's call took his life on a difficult Path. Diagnosed with chronic kidney disease, Hutchins tells PATH MEGAzine that he needed a new kidney soon or he could die. Placed immediately on dialysis, Hutchins shared the diagnosis with the church that he founded. That day 30 people stood up during service and volunteered to get tested to see if they were a donor match for the "God's Got A Blessing, With Your Name on It" singer.

One of those getting tested was Norman's own wife, Karen Hutchins. Not only was Karen a match, the Belize native was told by doctors that there was a one and 2.5-million-person chance that she was a perfect match. After beating the odds, Karen didn't hesitate to share the vital organ with her ailing husband. Says Pastor Hutchins, "I'm just grateful to God that my wife would be willing to donate me a kidney, and extend my life." Knowing that God's favor was on the couple, the couple would face a risky transplant, and complications that threatened to take his life as recently as just a few weeks ago.

Seemingly out of trouble, Hutchins' body

was responding to the kidney well, and Karen was quickly recovering. Anxiously claiming a complete healing, Hutchins soon found himself short of breath and later found out that his lungs were 90% filled up with fluid. Doctors quickly told Hutchins that he must undergo another procedure to drain the fluid that was literally causing him to drown. It was during the follow up operation that Pastor Hutchins' storied career that has impacted the lives of so many nearly came to an end.

Hutchins flat lined while doctors operated. Doctors went to get Norman's wife Karen (who was still in a wheel chair recovering) and she began to pray for her husband's life with oil. While Norman's wife and sisters looked on, doctors were frantically searching for solutions. After a few tense moments a nurse emphatically says, "We have a pulse!" With relief spreading across the face of those around, doctors were able to succeed in getting the fluid out, and now hoped the Pastor didn't sustain any brain damage. Doctors succeeded in stabilizing Hutchins 16 hours later.

During the interview Pastor rejoices, "I went in for one miracle and I came out with 5 miracles! The first miracle was that the transplant worked as soon as they put it [kidney] in. The second miracle is I didn't drown in the fluids; my lungs were 90% full. The third miracle is I flat lined. I was dead for two whole minutes, and God brought me back to life! And the fourth miracle is I didn't have any brain damage. And the fifth miracle was in 16 hours, God turned the whole situation around, and I was up and moving about and began to recover."

This wasn't the only time Hutchins had a brush with serious medical ailments. During doctor visits for his kidney transplant, doctors discovered that the singer had an undiagnosed mild heart attack that they believe happened at some point. Pastor Hutchins also battled bouts of acute blindness years ago due to complications with diabetes he's battled since childhood.

After 6 months of living and preaching blind, Pastor says he remembered God told him, "This is going to be the last day anybody leads you down this aisle." Hutchins tells Path Magazine's Kris Patrick, "It was one week after that date that God began to restore my sight."

It was at this point in Hutchins' testimony that we gained insight on how he overcomes obstacles. "A lot of times we ask the question why me? My response to that is why not you? Can you think of somebody else that you would wish that on other than yourself… Why not you?" Hutchins elaborates, "God will always do one of two things. Either He will deliver you from it, or He will give you the grace to go through it, and either way is victory."

Before the transplant and while on dialysis, Pastor Hutchins described his lowest point when the enemy began to come harder after his faith and will to survive. Pastor said in his subconscious the enemy said, "Look at you…You the preacher. You been preaching all these years about how faithful God is, and He's the healer, but look at you sitting up here in the chair getting dialysis. Where's your God now?" Pastor said he fought the attack, by realizing it could be worse. "The lady next to me has an oxygen tank that she has to carry with her everyday [on dialysis], but I don't."

It was such reasoning that lifted the spirits of Pastor during those lonely treatments. Pastor Hutchins says, "There's some things that God allows you to go through, because there's a level of grace you would have never known." Later in the interview Hutchins was moved to tears, "I thank God that in the midst of all of this, I've seen His mighty power; I've seen His hand."

At an early age Pastor Hutchins knew what he wanted to do. He began preaching at eight years old, and became an ordained minister at only twelve. It was at that tender age that Hutchins began touring the country preaching to packed-out congregations; standing on boxes so he could be seen over the podium.

Confident that he still has more to give to the Christian community Pastor Hutchins states, "The fact that He [God] brought me back to life tells me that He's not finished with me…That my work is not done."

Hutchins plans to continue to preach and record new music next year when the doctor clears him to travel. He shared with PATH MEGAzine that he is currently working on a deal with a new label, and says God is continuing to give him ideas for songs.

Pastor Hutchins says that his health is improving, and asks you to keep him and his family in your prayers. After following the call of God for over 48 years, I think we can all agree that this time Pastor Hutchins, 'God's got a blessing with YOUR name on it." [End of article]

Psalm 72:19
And blessed be his glorious name for ever: and let the whole earth be filled with his glory; Amen, and Amen.

Glory can be seen in God's beauty, power or honor. It is also a quality of God's character that emphasizes His greatness and authority. While God's glory is not a substance, at times God does reveal His perfection to man in a visible way. Such a display of the presence of God is often seen as fire or dazzling light, but sometimes as an act of power.

Some examples from the Old Testament are the pillar of cloud and fire (Exodus 13:21), the Lord's deliverance of the Israelites at the Red Sea (Exodus 14), and especially His glory in the tabernacle (Leviticus 9:23-24) and Temple (1 Kings 8:11). Since the close of the Old Testament, the glory of God has been shown mainly in Christ (Luke 9:29-32) and in the members of His church.

Christ now shares His divine glory with His followers, so that their lives are transformed into the glorious image of God. At the end of time in God's heavenly presence, Believers will be fully glorified. There, the glory of God will be seen everywhere (Revelation 21:23).

The word "glory" is used in three senses in the Bible:

1. God's moral beauty and perfection of character.
2. God's moral beauty and perfection as a visible presence.
3. The honor and audible praise which His creatures give to Him.

Praise is an act of worship or acknowledgment that recognizes and extols the virtues or deeds of another. The praise of man toward God is how we express our joy to the Lord. We are to praise God both for who He is and for what He does. Praising God for who He is, is called adoration. Praising Him for what He does, is known as thanksgiving. A godly person will echo David's words, "My praise shall be continually of you... And I will praise you yet more and more" (Psalm 71:6(b), 14(b) NASB).

Glory also can be seen in a form of worship that is characterized by reverent devotion and allegiance pledged to God; and, the rituals or ceremonies by which this reverence is expressed. The English word *worship* comes from the Old English word *worth ship*, a word which denotes the worthiness of the one receiving the special honor or devotion. The most powerful thing about this kind of worship, is that when you send it up as a form of glory, it comes back down in the form of manifestations of the power of God, and when His power comes down, everything that He is comes down. That means, whatever you need will be within reach. Hallelujah!

CHAPTER 4
Breaking the Spirit of Religion

Let us begin this chapter by exploring the birthplace of religion. Would it surprise you if I said God did not create religion? He desires a relationship; however, religion was created by man as an attempt to correct his unrighteous act of disobedience.

After Adam and Eve disobeyed a direct command from God not to partake of the tree in the midst of the garden, sin was introduced into the earth. After they partook of the forbidden fruit, their eyes were opened, and they saw their nakedness. Adam's attempt to correct the situation led him to sew the fig leaves to cover their bodies, but the reason this act could not correct the wrong that had been done was because no blood had been shed.

Genesis 3:7
And the eyes of them both were opened, and they knew that they were naked; and they sewed fig leaves together, and made themselves aprons.

For Adam, religion was his attempt to clothe himself apart from the righteousness of God. In modern times, we create religion through the fig leaves of church attendance, singing in the choir, serving as a greeter, and any other servitude without being washed in the blood of the lamb. These are examples of false religion. But true religion is the belief in and reverence for God.

Colossians 2:8
Beware lest any man spoil you through philosophy and vain deceit, after the tradition of men, after the rudiments of the world, and not after Christ.

One of the ways we can begin to break the spirit of false religion, is for the body of Christ to refrain from teaching doctrine that does not require one to have a proper relationship with God. An example of this would be, if you teach it is wrong for a woman to wear pants or red lipstick, and it is not endorsed by the Scriptures, that would be false religion.

I remember at Frontline Ministries, we did a Bible Study series on "Breaking the Spirit of Religion." We dealt with doctrines that have been taught through the years at churches that did not have the support of the Scriptures. Often, these doctrines were formulated through customs, culture, and personal beliefs. True religion can only be true when the Scriptures endorse it.

One of the things we did in that Bible Study series was to ask anyone who had a question about a doctrinal practice to write it down in a sealed note and place it in a certain box. For about five weeks we pulled questions out of the box and let the Scriptures validate the claim of whether a doctrine was false religion or true religion, based on the revelation of God's Word.

I have chosen a few of the doctrines we discussed to share with you in this book. Hopefully some of these areas will free you to live, and not be confined to a system of rules and regulations implemented by man. I will share the question, and then explore the related Scripture.

1. Question: Is it a sin to wear tattoos?
Leviticus 19:28

Ye shall not make any cuttings in your flesh for the dead, nor print any marks upon you: I am the Lord.

Some say that getting a tattoo is a sin, because in Leviticus, the Bible forbids placing any type of mark on the body.

With a simple reading of this verse, it appears that tattoos are clearly forbidden in the Bible. However, while it's true that tattoos were forbidden under Levitical law, we must remember that these laws were given to the Nation of Israel, not the Body of Christ. As Christians, not all of the laws given to Israel apply to us. In the Old Testament, God gave moral, civil and ceremonial laws. For Christians, the moral law (The Ten Commandments) remains in effect to direct our moral judgment and to command us to obey God.

While the law has no power to save us, it certainly has power to direct our lives by guiding us to make godly choices to avoid sin and to live in a way that honors God. The Ten Commandments reflect the very nature of God, His perfection and His righteousness.

We can never attain the perfection God's law commands, but we can live our lives moving in that direction. Jesus magnified the Ten

Commandments, the moral law, during His earthly ministry and Paul confirmed this law for the Church. God does not change, nor does His moral law change. Therefore, we are called to obey the Ten Commandments.

The ceremonial and civil laws were given to the Nation of Israel. As a whole, these laws are not binding on Christians, although many of them are good for our instruction and our sanctification. We find many repeated in the New Testament as directives for Christian living (e.g. restitution for wrongdoing). The ceremonial and civil laws were given to Israel to instruct them how to live in relationship with God and to keep them separate from other nations and holy unto God.

The prohibition for tattoos in Leviticus 19 falls under the ceremonial laws given to the Nation of Israel. The body markings and tattoos, during that time, were symbols of pagan worship or identification with other gods and nations. Israel was clearly told to avoid such markings of their flesh, but there is no such prohibition given to Christians.

The simple answer is…it depends. It depends on the motivation behind the decision to get a tattoo, the image of the tattoo, and what it might "say" to others. So, the answer is really not very simple at all.

This is a question that requires personal discernment using biblical instruction. A Christian knows that they have liberty in Christ Jesus, but with this liberty comes great responsibility. But to outright say that if a person has a tattoo they cannot be saved or go to heaven, would be false religion.

2. Question: Is it a sin to masturbate, i.e. sexual gratification through self-stimulation?

The Bible nowhere specifically forbids or denounces masturbation. It does, of course, denounce all forms of sexual impurity and fantasies that would involve adulterous relationships whether actual or mental. The problem with masturbation is that it not only can become habit forming and addictive, but men and women often engage in pornography and adulterous fantasies in order to reach a climax.

The difference in sex drive in a couple is often not the real problem or issue. It is rather a breakdown in the relationship and in an understanding of the role of sex in marriage as that which not only gives pleasure but expresses love, unity, and commitment to each other.

Masturbation has a tendency to isolate its

captives psychologically and socially. In masturbation, the person is focused on himself or herself alone, even though he or she usually is fantasizing about someone else at the same time. It is impossible for the one who is practicing this habit to experience the full extent of sexual emotions.

Along with the act of masturbation comes the fantasy of the mind. When practiced often, a pattern or cycle seems to become established within the individual's mind. Thus, perversion has a tendency to control the mind and this in- turn initiates the act. The real danger lies in your own mind and increases as the individual dwells in this world of fantasy.

3. Question: Do you have to be baptized to go to heaven?

To find the biblical answer to this question, we will look at two stories in the New Testament that will enable us to "reason" from Scripture. We will find truth there that can be applied to this issue.

The first story is found in Luke 16 and it is the account of the rich man and the beggar Lazarus. *"The time came when the beggar died and the angels carried him to Abraham's side. The rich man also died and was buried"* (Luke 16:22). Notice that there was no rite of baptism that was necessary to open Abraham's bosom for this beggar. This is of course before the LORD Jesus' death and resurrection, but baptism was a rite practiced by the Jews long before Jesus came to earth.

In fact, the baptism of John the Baptist was for the Jews and was not for salvation, but for repentance. Since this was a story that was told by Jesus, if it had been necessary for the beggar to be baptized to get into the place of rest, would not Jesus have added that information to the story? The rite of baptism in the New Testament was to identify the believer and to set them apart as a part of the "way" of Christ.

The other story is found in the account of Jesus on the cross and it is the story of one of the malefactors who hung beside Jesus. One of the malefactors railed against Jesus but the other had a change of heart. *"But the other criminal rebuked him. 'Don't you fear God,' he said, 'since you are under the same sentence? We are punished justly, for we are getting what our deeds deserve. But this man has done nothing wrong.' Then he said, 'Jesus, remember me when you come into your kingdom.' Jesus answered him, 'I tell you the truth, today you will be with me in paradise.'"*

Notice that Jesus does not say you will be with me after you are baptized. Rather there was affirmation of the thought "absent from the body and present with the LORD" (2 Corinthians 5:8).

The Purpose for Baptism

Water baptism is a picture of the Gospel, showing the death, burial and resurrection of Jesus Christ. We are baptized not to be saved but because we are saved. There is no salvation in baptism. Salvation comes through repentance, asking Jesus Christ to forgive you of your sins and accepting Him as your Savior.

Romans 10:9
That if thou shalt confess with thy mouth the Lord Jesus, and shalt believe in thine heart that God hath raised him from the dead, thou shalt be saved.

We are encouraged to be baptized in water as a public confession to all who witness that we have been born again. Being immersed in water is symbolic of dying and coming back to life, but this new life is in Christ Jesus. Although baptism is not required for one's salvation, every new believer is encouraged to do so, to be an outward witness of your inward conviction.

2 Corinthians 5:17
Therefore if any man be in Christ, he is a new creature: old things are passed away; behold, all things are become new.

4. Question: Is drinking a sin?

It is not a sin to drink alcohol in moderation. The Bible describes wine as a gift from God that can make life more enjoyable (Psalm 104:14-15; Ecclesiastes 3:13; 9:7). The Bible also acknowledges the medicinal value of wine (1 Timothy 5:23).

Jesus drank wine during His time on earth (Matthew 26:29; Luke 7:34). In one of His well-known miracles, Jesus turned water into wine as a generous gift at a marriage feast (John 2:1-10).

Dangers of Overdrinking

While the Bible mentions the positive aspects of wine, it condemns overdrinking and drunkenness. Thus, a Christian who chooses to drink alcohol would do so only in moderation (1 Timothy 3:8; Titus 2:2, 3). The Bible gives several reasons to avoid overdrinking.

- It impairs thinking ability and judgment (Proverbs 23:29-35). An intoxicated person cannot fulfill the Bible's command to "present your bodies as a living sacrifice, holy and acceptable to God, a sacred service with your power of reason" (Romans 12:1).

- Overdrinking removes inhibitions

and "the motivation to do what is right" (Hosea 4:11; Ephesians 5:18).
• It can lead to poverty and serious health problems (Proverbs 23:21, 31, 32).
• Heavy drinking and drunkenness displease God (Proverbs 23:20; Galatians 5:19-21).

How much is too much?

A person has had too much alcohol when his drinking puts him or others at risk of harm. According to the Bible, drunkenness is identified, not by a person's passing out, but by such behavior as being disoriented, walking unsteadily, becoming contentious, or having slurred speech (Job 12:25; Psalm 107:27; Proverbs 23:29-30, 33). Even those who avoid getting drunk can still become 'weighed down with... heavy drinking' and experience serious consequences (Luke 21:34-35).

The Bible also identifies times when Christians should avoid drinking alcohol altogether:
• If your drinking would cause others to stumble (Romans 14:21).

• If drinking alcohol violates the law of the land (Romans 13:1).

• If a person cannot control his drinking. Those who suffer from alcoholism and other forms of alcohol abuse must be willing to take drastic action (Matthew 5:29, 30).

Personally, I just stay away from it, so that the enemy will not have an opportunity to get the advantage over me!

5. Question: Is smoking a sin?

The Bible never directly mentions smoking. There are principles; however, that definitely apply to smoking. First, the Bible commands us not to allow our bodies to become "mastered" by anything. "Everything is permissible for me but not everything is beneficial. Everything is permissible for me, but I will not be mastered by anything" (1 Corinthians 6:12).

Smoking is undeniably strongly addictive. Later in the same passage we are told, *"Do you not know that your body is a temple of the Holy Spirit, who is in you, whom you have received from God? You are not your own; you were bought at a price. Therefore honor God with your body"* (1 Corinthians 6:19-20). Smoking is undoubtedly very bad for your health. It has been proven to damage the lungs and the heart.

6. Question: Does the Bible say anything about sex?

Rather than prohibit sexual pleasure, the Bible

shows that it is a gift from God to married people. He created humans "male and female" and viewed what he had made as being "very good" (Genesis 1:27, 31). When He brought the first man and woman together in marriage, He said that "they must become one flesh" (Genesis 2:24). This bond included the pleasure of sexual intimacy along with a close emotional connection.

The Bible describes the pleasure that husbands find in marriage with these words: *"Rejoice with the wife of your youth. . . Let her own breasts intoxicate you at all times. With her love may you be in an ecstasy constantly"* (Proverbs 5:18, 19). God also intends for wives to enjoy sex. The Bible says, *"Husbands and wives should satisfy each other's sexual needs"* (1 Corinthians 7:3, God's Word Bible).

God reserves sexual relations for marriage mates only, as Hebrews 13:4 shows, *"Let marriage be honorable among all, and the marriage bed be without defilement, for God will judge fornicators and adulterers."* Married couples must be faithful and maintain their commitment to each other. They find the greatest delight, not by pursuing selfish gratification, but by applying the biblical principle: *"There is more happiness in giving than there is in receiving"* (Acts 20:35).

CHAPTER 5
DEVELOPING FIVE SPIRITUAL HABITS

A habit is an automatic pattern of behavior in reaction to a specific situation, also an established custom. Bad habits should always be broken, but there are five spiritual habits that every believer should develop to ensure a proper relationship with God. When spiritual habits become a part of your lifestyle and your daily routine, one of the benefits is that you will always be in alignment with God's Word.

Spiritual habits help you to become spiritually sound, which in return will help you develop sound character. In this chapter, we will discuss five spiritual habits that are supported by the Scriptures that will help you to be spiritually fit at all times.

You should always be equipped for the unexpected attacks from the enemy, but sometimes life just happens, and your response will often determine the outcome. These five spiritual habits will help you not to make a mess out of a mess. If you have not already developed these five spiritual habits, I urge you to start working on them now. One of my philosophies is, it's better to have it and not need it, rather to need it and not have it.

First Spiritual Habit
"Be Sound in Speech"

Proverbs 18:21
Death and life are in the power of the tongue: and they that love it shall eat the fruit thereof.

In this text, the word *tongue* means speech or words that we speak; the word *fruit* means harvest. Putting them both together, we understand that our harvest comes from the fruit of our words. "Life and death are in the power of the tongue" means you have a choice. You can either speak death to your life, or you can speak life to your life, because your words have power. What we speak is a picture of what's in our heart.

Matthew 12:35-36
A good man out of the good treasure of the heart bringeth forth good things: and an evil man out of the evil treasure bringeth forth evil things.

The confession of your faith comes from the words that you speak. An example of the power of words can be seen in the resurrection of Jesus Christ. The first question is, did Jesus die? And of course, the answer is, Yes, He did! Now remember in the Scriptures, He said, when you *"Destroy this temple, I will raise it up again in three days"* (John 2:19b, NIRV). Jesus used the words I will. But how can a dead man raise himself up if he's dead? There was no life in His body! But earlier, before He died, remember He said, "When you destroy this body…"

Jesus put His words in the atmosphere before He died! So, when he was dead, even though He could not raise Himself up, His Word had to obey his command! So He got up! In essence, He did raise Himself up, but it was from the words that He put in the atmosphere.

He has given to us that same kind of authority. Even though we do not see the manifestation of our words right now, we must put them in the atmosphere. God's Word will not return unto Him void.

Isaiah 55:11-12
So shall my word be that goeth forth out of my mouth: it shall not return unto me void, but it shall accomplish that which I please, and it shall prosper in the thing whereto I sent it.

Real faith is not speaking what you see; it is speaking what you do not see, speaking what you believe. Your belief should not be rooted in what you want, but it should be rooted in what God said. Therefore, you must speak by faith even if you can't see it.

Your words are not based on the evidence of what you can see, even though the facts are real. Faith says, "The facts have to bow down to the faith of my words".

2 Corinthians 4:18
While we look not at the things which are seen, but at the things which are not seen: for the things which are seen are temporal; but the things which are not seen are eternal.

Words are like seeds, and when they are planted in the soil of your mind, the manifestation, whether good or bad, will be the harvest. Making sound speech one of your habits is a daily growing process. The moment you recognize the words in your mouth have no value to the success and the manifestation of your visions, dreams, purpose and destiny, you will change to fruitful words.

Ephesians 4:29
Let no corrupt communication proceed out of your mouth, but that which is good to the use of edifying, that it may minister grace unto the hearers.

The more you speak fruitful words and words of life to yourself, the sooner you will develop a spiritual habit of sound speech. As a matter of fact, use this Scripture as practical therapy:

Deuteronomy 28:3,6
³ Blessed shalt thou be in the city, and blessed shalt thou be in the field.
⁶ Blessed shalt thou be when thou comest in, and blessed shalt thou be when thou goest out.

Second Spiritual Habit
"Be Sound in Faith"

Romans 1:17
For therein is the righteousness of God revealed from faith to faith: as it is written, the just shall live by faith.

The just shall live by faith. Who are the just? They are those who have been justified by the blood of Jesus Christ. To be justified is to have the legal guilt of sin removed from your life. Through the death, burial, and resurrection of Jesus Christ, you were justified. One of the reasons Christians must live by faith is because our salvation can only come through faith.

Ephesians 2:8
For by grace are ye saved through faith; and that not of yourselves: it is the gift of God.

If you take God at His word for your salvation, then you must take Him at His word for every promise in the Scriptures thereafter. When the text says, "from faith to faith," it is primarily talking about how your faith grows. For the just, faith is a lifestyle.

One text says, "the just shall live by faith" and the other says, we are "saved through faith." These scriptures reference two different things. To be "saved through faith" is to believe in the work of the cross; to "live by faith" is to take God at His word and trust in His promises on a daily basis.

1 John 3:22-23
And whatsoever we ask, we receive of him, because we keep his commandments, and do those things that are pleasing in his sight.

Third Spiritual Habit

"Be Sound in the Word"

Ephesians 1:17-18
¹⁷ That the God of our Lord Jesus Christ, the Father of glory, may give unto you the spirit of wisdom and revelation in the knowledge of him:
¹⁸ The eyes of your understanding being enlightened; that ye may know what is the hope of his calling, and what the riches of the glory of his inheritance in the saints,

When the text says that the Father "may give unto you the spirit of wisdom and revelation in the knowledge of Him," this refers to wisdom as the end result of knowledge and revelation. If we were to put them in a chronological order, it would be knowledge first, then wisdom and then revelation.

If you do not have knowledge, there can be no revelation or wisdom. You must acquire knowledge first. Knowledge is to know and learn God's Word; to memorize it, and be able to recall Scriptures. In the book of Hosea 4:6, it says, "My people are destroyed for the lack of knowledge." Notice what it did not say; it did not say for the lack of wisdom, or the lack of revelation. Because there can be no revelation or wisdom of a thing where there is no knowledge of a thing.

A good example would be the stop sign. Let's just say for the sake of explaining the difference between knowledge, revelation and wisdom, you knew nothing about a stop sign. So, when you saw it for the first time, you asked what is this? If I respond by telling you that it is a stop sign, that is knowledge, but you have no revelation or wisdom yet. If I ask you, after you acquired knowledge of what it is, you would say, "It is a stop sign." But if I only gave you knowledge and no revelation about the stop sign, you would not be able to answer my next questions: "What is a stop sign? and, "What is it for?"

On the other hand, if I gave you knowledge and then revelation about the stop sign, you would be able to tell me that when you get to the sign, you must stop and look in every direction before you move, to make sure the path is clear. Now you have knowledge and revelation, and as you process your knowledge and revelation of the stop sign, here comes wisdom, the ability to make sound judgment based on the knowledge and revelation you've received.

So, when you come to the stop sign, you have a choice. Do I stop first, or just drive past? If you make the wrong choice, it can cost you your life. In the same way, if you had no knowledge of what the sign means, it still could cost you your life. So, when the text says we are destroyed for the lack of knowledge, it is because where there is no knowledge, there can be no revelation or wisdom. That's why Satan will always make sure you are too busy to get the knowledge of God's Word. He will cause your life to be so distracted, that studying and memorizing God's Word is almost impossible. Yet, in the Scriptures, we are not just encouraged, but we are commanded by God to know the Word of God.

2 Timothy 2:15
Study to shew thyself approved unto God,
a workman that needeth not to be ashamed,
rightly dividing the word of truth.

To be sound in the Word is not only to know what it says, but to understand the revelation of it. When you are confronted with life's challenges, the Word of God dictates how you will respond, and your course of action will be governed by the wisdom of the revelation of the knowledge you have received.

The only thing left to do now is get busy learning God's Word. The revelation of God's Word will become clearer to you as you learn to know it, because it is the job of the Holy Spirit to illuminate God's Word to every believer.

Wisdom will be your choice of what to do with the knowledge and revelation you receive. I encourage you to create a systematic pattern of studying and getting to know God's Word, because wisdom is waiting for you! Here are some familiar Scriptures to memorize:

Philippians 4:19
But my God shall supply all your need according to his riches in glory by Christ Jesus.

Matthew 6:33-34
33 But seek ye first the kingdom of God, and his righteousness; and all these things shall be added unto you.
34 Take therefore no thought for the morrow: for the morrow shall take thought for the things of itself. Sufficient unto the day is the evil thereof.

Mark 11:24
Therefore I say unto you, What things soever ye desire, when ye pray, believe that ye receive them, and ye shall have them.

John 15:7
If ye abide in me, and my words abide in you, ye shall ask what ye will, and it shall be done unto you.

Fourth Spiritual Habit

"Be Sound in Prayer"

Philippians 4:6
Be careful for nothing; but in everything by prayer and supplication with thanksgiving let your requests be made known unto God.

For the Christian, praying is supposed to be like breathing, easier to do than not to do. We pray for a variety of reasons. For one thing, prayer is a form of serving God and obeying Him. We pray because God commands us to pray.

If Jesus thought it was worthwhile to pray, we should, too. If He needed to pray to remain in the Father's will, how much more do we need to pray? Another reason to pray is that God intends prayer to be the means of obtaining His solutions in a number of situations. We pray in preparation for major decisions to overcome demonic forces, to gather workers for the spiritual harvest, to gain strength to overcome temptation, and to obtain the means of strengthening others spiritually

Ephesians 6:18
Praying always with all prayer and supplication in the Spirit, and watching thereunto with all perseverance and supplication for all saints;

When we come to God with our specific requests, we have God's promise that our prayers are not in vain, even if we do not receive specifically what we ask for. He has promised that when we ask for things that are in accordance with His will, He will give us what we ask for.

1 John 5:14
And this is the confidence that we have in him, that, if we ask any thing according to his will, he heareth us:

Sometimes, He delays His answers according to His wisdom and for our benefit. In these situations, we are to be diligent and persistent in prayer. Prayer should not be seen as our means of getting God to do our will on earth, but rather, as a means of getting God's will done on earth.

God's wisdom far exceeds our own; therefore, always pray His will be done.

For situations in which we do not know God's will specifically, prayer is a means of discerning His will. If the Syrian woman with the demon-influenced daughter had not prayed to Christ, her daughter would not have been made whole. If the blind man outside Jericho had not called out to Christ, he would have remained blind. God has said that we often go without because we do not ask. In one sense, prayer is like sharing the Gospel with people. We do not know who will respond to the message of the Gospel until we share it. In the same way, we will never see the results of answered prayer unless we pray.

A lack of prayer demonstrates a lack of faith and a lack of trust in God's Word. We pray to demonstrate our faith in God, that He will do as He has promised in His Word and bless our lives abundantly more than we could ask or hope for.

Prayer is our primary means of seeing God work in others' lives. Because it is our means of "plugging into" God's power, it is our means of defeating Satan and his army, which we are powerless to overcome by ourselves.

Therefore, may God find us often before His throne; for we have a high priest in heaven that can identify with all that we go through. We have His promise that the fervent prayer of a righteous man accomplishes much.

James 5:16
The effectual fervent prayer of a righteous man availeth much.

Fifth Spiritual Habit
"Be Sound in Praise"

Psalm 100:4
Enter into his gates with thanksgiving, and into his courts with praise: be thankful unto him, and bless his name.

Notice in our text you see the words *thanksgiving and praise*. Both words mean the same thing, but there is a slight difference in the approach.

When the writer says, "Enter into his gates with thanksgiving," thanksgiving means adoration. We give thanks and praise to God for who He is, and not just for what He does. The second word, praise in the text means to thank Him for what He has done. Praise cannot be silent; even the Hebrew words for praise invite us to be vocal.

Psalm 34:1-3
I will bless the Lord at all times: his praise shall continually be in my mouth.
² My soul shall make her boast in the Lord: the humble shall hear thereof, and be glad.
³ O magnify the Lord with me, and let us exalt his name together.

The Bible commands all living creatures to praise the Lord in Psalm 150:6. One Hebrew word for "praise" is *yadah*, meaning "praise, give thanks, or confess." A second word often translated "praise" in the Old Testament is *zamar*, "sing praise." A third word translated "praise" is *halal* (the root of *hallelujah*), meaning "to praise, honor, or commend." All three terms contain the idea of giving thanks and honor to one who is worthy of praise.

The book of Psalms is a collection of songs filled with praises to God. Among them is Psalm 9, which says, *"I will be glad and rejoice in you; I will sing the praises of your name, O Most High."* Psalm 18:3 says, God is *"worthy of praise."* Psalm 21:13 praises God both for who He is and for His great power. *"Be thou exalted, LORD, in thine own strength: so will we sing and praise thy power."*

Psalm 150 uses the term *praise* thirteen times in six verses. The first verse provides the "where" of praise…everywhere! *"Praise God in his sanctuary; praise him in his mighty heavens."* The next verse teaches "why" to praise the Lord: *"Praise him for his acts of power; praise him for his surpassing greatness."* Verses 3–6 notes "how" to praise the Lord—with a variety of instruments, dance, and everything that has breath.

In the New Testament, there are examples of praise given to Jesus. In Matthew 21:16 it refers to those who praised Jesus as He rode a donkey into Jerusalem. Matthew 8:2 notes a leper who bowed before Jesus. In Matthew 28:17, the disciples of Jesus were said to worship Him after His resurrection. Jesus accepted praise as God.

The early church often shared in times of praise. For example, the first church in Jerusalem included a focus on worship in Acts 2:42–43. The church leaders at Antioch prayed, worshiped, and fasted during the time Paul and Barnabas were called into missionary work. Many of Paul's letters include extended sections of praise to the Lord.

Isaiah 61:3
To appoint unto them that mourn in Zion, to give unto them beauty for ashes, the oil of joy for mourning, the garment of praise for the spirit of heaviness; that they might be called trees of righteousness, the planting of the Lord, that he might be glorified.

CHAPTER 6
Trusting God Through Difficult Times

That ye may be the children of your Father which is in heaven: for he maketh his sun to rise on the evil and on the good, and sendeth rain on the just and on the unjust.
-Matthew 5:45-46

Being a born again believer, does not exempt you from trouble, trials and adversities. That's why the Scripture says, 'it rains on the just as well as the unjust.' It rains on the saved and the unsaved. But I can testify that it's a different kind of rain!

When you are walking with God, no matter what you experience, according to the Scriptures, *"And we know that all things work together for good to them that love God, to them who are the called according to his purpose" (Romans 8:28).*

One thing I have learned through every challenge that I have faced, is that your faith is perfected in your trial, and your revelation of God becomes clearer. It is hard to see the value of a trial while you're going through it, but when you come out, the lessons that you have learned are invaluable.

In the early part of January 2005, I remember waking up early one morning and things not looking the same. Straight lines were crooked and things appeared to be further away from me than they really were. Frightened and confused, I went to the eye doctor to find out what was going on.

After my eye examination, the doctor was hysterical. He said, "We need to get you to the emergency room now! Both of your retinas are detaching!" Not understanding the severity of what he had just said, my response to him was, "I've got to go do a concert. Can I get it checked when I come back?" He replied to me, "You will be blind by the time you get back." That's when my heart fell to the bottom of my stomach. They rushed me to a hospital in Maryland and I remember them rolling me down the hallway. On my way to the operating room, I was just praying, "Lord please do not let me go blind."

Just the thought of not being able to see was terrifying!

Before they put me under the anesthesia, the doctor explained that they were going to put me in a "twilight sleep," meaning I would be asleep, but not in a deep sleep. It would be possible for me to hear and see various things.

I remember waking up during surgery. I could hear things, but I could not see the doctors. I saw the instruments that they were using in my eyes but I could not feel anything. I could see images, which reminded me of Star Wars. Then I dozed off. After several hours of surgery, I woke up and I must tell you there are no words to describe what I felt in the first few seconds because at that moment, I discovered I was completely blind!

The truth is, I thought that in the first five minutes I was going to lose my mind! To hear the doctor talk to me; to hear my wife speak to me and not be able to see them or have any sense of where I was, was almost more than I could bear. At that moment, the only thing that brought me comfort was quoting faith Scriptures to myself and singing songs of healing.

I recall my wife driving me home, which took about an hour and a half. I had no sense of direction. I could hear the cars on the road, and an airplane flying overhead; I could hear the sound of music from other cars when we would stop at a red light. All I kept thinking to myself was, How did this happen to me?

As my wife drove, she kept speaking life to me and encouraging me that this was not going to last forever.

I felt so helpless as a man, not being physically able to protect my wife; not to mention the thousands of questions that were going through my mind. How would I work? How would I preach? How would I pastor the church?

After arriving home, my wife guided me into the house. From there, I felt my way through every room. One of the challenges ahead was my studio. How would I work the equipment? How would I continue to write music? So many questions and thoughts in my mind, but I never blamed God and I never felt that He had forsaken me. Actually, I blamed myself because my blindness was caused from the complications of diabetes which I allowed to get out of control. The price for not being disciplined was my sight.

It was at that moment I repented to God for not taking better care of myself and I vowed to Him that if He would restore my sight, I would do better. I recall Him speaking to me through the Holy Spirit and saying it in love, "I am chastising you. Norman, you are no good to me spiritually if you do not take care of yourself naturally. Because of your assignment, I'm going to restore your sight." At that moment, I had no idea how long it would be, but the highlight of my day became bedtime because I had an expectancy that maybe tomorrow would be the day I'd see again.

I remember at dinner time my wife did not spoon feed me. Instead she would put the plate in front of me and give me instructions. "Your baked chicken is at 12 o'clock, your rice is at 3 o'clock, and your green beans are at 6 o'clock." She never treated me as though I was blind. Through the whole ordeal, I experienced nothing from her but faith in action. Each passing day became more challenging to me because my mind was trying to convince me that this was how it would be the rest of my life.

I called a pastor friend from Texas to share with him what had happened. After telling him the whole story, he said, "Man you can't see nothing?!"

I replied, "I can't see my hand in front of my face." Then he asked me the strangest question. "But can you still preach?" And when he said that to me, I found my fight. I said, "You're right! I may be blind, but I can still preach."

I had my wife read the Scriptures to me, then I would record them in my mind, since I was without vision. Next, I would rehearse the Scriptures that I had heard through the week and have them memorized by Sunday.

After almost a week, we felt it was time to let the church know. First, I called a meeting with the deacons and when they saw me, I could hear them saying, "My God, what happened to Pastor?" I could even hear some of them crying after explaining to them what happened. I suggested that we go to the church and practice me walking to the pulpit. This was Saturday before the second Sunday in January of 2005. I will never forget that Sunday morning when I walked into the church with my hand on one of the deacon's shoulders as he walked me down the aisle to my seat.

As we walked down the aisle, I could hear the Saints saying, "Is Pastor blind? Oh my God, what happened?" Then I heard nothing but crying and groaning. I could not see the facial expressions of the members, but I could feel their hurt and dismay. At that moment, I wanted to go back home. I guess because the house had become my comfort zone. There, I had a sense of security and familiarity because I could walk through the house with no help.

To compensate for my lack of vision, when it was time for me to preach, the deacon guided me to the pulpit. The first thing I did was repent to the congregation as I explained to them how this happened. I remember preaching from the subject, *Trusting God Through Difficult Times*. I shared with them what God said to me about restoring my sight.

So, every week I preached and every day I worked in the administrative offices and still did counseling. I learned how to dial my phone without seeing it. I kept up with all my meetings, and by Sunday, I was ready to preach again. I was preaching to the congregation, but I was really preaching faith to myself.

During this period of blindness, I had about three different operations, but none of them led to any real success. After the last surgery, I asked the doctor, "Just be honest with me. Will I ever see again?"

He replied, "Preacher, don't you believe in miracles?" That made me put on my war face and I was like, "devil bring it on!" As a result, some of the biggest songs of my career were written during that time.

Here's something funny that I remember. One morning we woke up and it was about six inches of snow outside. My wife was getting dressed to go outside to shovel the sidewalk and the driveway. Then I messed up and said, "I'm going to help." She never said, "How can you do that? You're blind." All she said was, "Okay."

I got dressed, put on my boots, my coat and my gloves. We went outside, and I said to her, "Give me a shovel and point me to the snow." I was shoveling snow and couldn't even see it. The funny thing was, I didn't realize I was shoveling my snow over the spots that she had just shoveled. But she never said anything because she knew it made me feel good to be helping. I felt like my old self again; I even had the nerve to try to have a snowball fight.

On another day, I was home by myself. My wife had gone out and I was in the studio working on a song. Some of the lyrics were, "Lord I want to dwell in your presence. That's where I want to be. I want to bask in your Spirit. That's where I want to be." Then suddenly, I was frightened because I felt like someone was in the house besides me. I remember screaming, "Whoever's in this house, you need to get out!"

Immediately, there was a peace that came over

me and the room lit up brightly. I could feel a peace in my spirit that I never felt before and at that moment, I wasn't afraid or nervous anymore. I felt the presence of God and I asked Him, "What is this I feel?" He said to me, "I'm giving you a glimpse of glory." I said to Him, "Lord, if I never see again, if I can just feel what I feel now, I'll be okay!"

I believe that's when I solidified my miracle.

Four months later, which made a total of six months of being blind; on the third Sunday of the month, I was at church preaching, and it was such an unusual day. I remember saying to those who had received Christ and had joined the church, "Stick around! I'll see you one day!" At that point, word had spread, and people were coming to hear this blind recording artist preacher preach.

On that special Sunday, I preached the sermon, "This is Not How My Story Ends!" At the end of the service, the Lord spoke to me and said, "This Sunday, today will be the last day anyone leads you down this aisle." I shared that with others, as well as my wife and we were all excited!

I thought my vision would return either that night or the next morning, but when I woke up, I was still blind. By Friday of that week, I was still without vision. My mind was now telling me, "Maybe what you thought you heard from God was really yourself." But I was doing my best not to believe what my mind was trying to convince me of.

Saturday came, and I was thinking, "I can't go to church tomorrow. I'm still blind. Maybe I'll give God another week."

I was getting ready to call one of the ministers to fill in for me, then I remembered the song that I had written. *If God said it, that settles it and that's good enough for me.* I made up my mind that I was going to church, vision or no vision. I decided to trust in what I knew God had said.

I went to bed that Saturday night blind, but when I woke up that Sunday morning, I saw something I had not seen in six months. I looked to my left and I could see a silhouette of my wife in bed. As I moved closer to her, I could see her face. I woke her up and said, "Honey I can see you!" *Hallelujah*! She jumped up and we started rejoicing.

My vision was still cloudy, and I couldn't tell who people were from a distance, but I could at least see well enough to walk and not bump into people. Needless to say, when we got to church that Sunday morning and I walked down that aisle by myself, it was a spiritual explosion at Frontline Ministries! And every day, little by little my vision began to return.

Today I drive, and can read without glasses and I walk down the aisle by myself. It has been 12 years now and I'm still walking in the miracle of God giving me my sight back. It rains on the just as well as the unjust, but for the just, it's a different kind of rain.

CHAPTER 7
MY JOSEPH STORY

And Joseph dreamed a dream, and he told it his brethren: and they hated him yet the more.
-Genesis 37:5

My childhood "Joseph Story" started when I was just six years old in a small town in the south. As I look back, I can say God's grace will find you no matter where you are.

It was 1962 in Kinston, North Carolina, and a boy child was born to Doris Hutchins, father unknown at the time. My mother had six boys and six girls. I was the baby boy, but I never really knew my brothers during my childhood. I remember seeing them but never really having an encounter or relationship with them. What is really amazing is we were poor, but I never knew that. I used to wonder why we were always moving to a different house every few months.

One day I came home from school and all our furniture was on the front lawn. I had no idea we had been evicted. Back then, the landlord could put your stuff out on the street.

I can still remember the fresh aroma of buttermilk biscuits, molasses and that thick bacon which was one of our regular dinners. We had a piano in the house and my mother played for several churches. Back then, I was not interested in the piano or any instruments. I was too busy just trying to survive and be noticed.

Amazingly, I remember my first day at kindergarten. My sister took me, and it was okay until she tried to leave. I cried, and I would not stop, so she stayed. Growing up, we never really went to church until we moved to Delaware. I didn't know why then, but now I know it was because we didn't have clothes. But every once in a while, mother would take us to church.

It was called Quarterly Meeting and I loved it. I could hear the preacher preach, the old-time choir, and not to mention all the good food we would have after the service. At home we didn't have a lot. The games or toys were the ones we made up. Actually, to this day, I still have some of them. As a child, I have no memories of playing any kind of games with my mother. I guess she was just so busy working and going to church.

I recall the truck she used to drive with all the people on the back of it. They would go to the field to crop tobacco. I was a child growing up in an adult world and a house full of people, yet I felt so alone. My escape was to daydream, something I could do for hours.

"Shush! Be quiet! He's home. I do all that I can just to stay out of his way. I don't know why he doesn't like me, and why he's so mean to me. I'm afraid of him, but I have nowhere to hide. He just called my name! Should I go, or should I stay? "Yes sir," I respond. It's the same routine. He's been drinking again. He's mad at my mother so he takes it out on me. I'm blamed for stuff I didn't do; I guess that justifies the beating."

We had a black-and-white television with only two channels, no HBO and no Showtime. Those networks were not invented yet. But I could daydream until the pain went away. It was Sunday morning and I really wanted to go to church. I was seven now, but my clothes looked too bad, so we had to stay home again. I was home alone with three of my sisters, who were in their own little worlds. Sometimes, I would sneak out the back door. They thought I was outside playing, but I would walk through a bushy path until I came upon the small church.

There was a strange sound coming from inside. I could hear the music playing, and the loud singing. As I drew closer, I could tell they were singing about God. I peeped in and saw what I thought were angels. There were about eight women dressed in white from head to toe. They were dancing, shouting and singing. It sounded good, too! A lady spotted me peeking into the window, and invited me inside.

I don't remember them ever asking me my name, but put me in a circle and prayed for me. As they prayed, it sounded like they were speaking a language from a different country. Now I know that they were speaking in tongues. I don't remember exactly what they prayed, but I was just glad to be noticed. The church building is still there to this day and I've seen it not long ago.

Now back to my Joseph Story. I knew I had to get back home because if he found out that I left the house without permission, I would be in big trouble. I hoped that whatever those women prayed would deliver me from him. Once somebody took the change off his dresser and we were all questioned.

"Somebody took it! If you don't tell me who did it, I'm beating all of you!" he said. No one came forward to confess, so we all lined up as usual. I was the last and of course whoever was last got the worst and longest beating. I got beat so many times for things I knew I hadn't done. Sometimes, I felt like I might as well do it anyway, but I was too afraid. Maybe this was the way he expressed his love for us, but there was something about it that just didn't feel right. I guess I was too young to understand.

It was Monday, a school day and I was in second grade. "Can somebody please help me? I can't read." Everybody was too busy, so I had to find a way to pretend to keep from being embarrassed. "Can you show me how to do that math again? I'm sorry I don't understand. I think it's hard for me to concentrate and think."

I was thinking about what was going to happen when I got home.

Would he be drunk again? What would he hit me with this time, a closed fist or an extension cord? I just didn't know, and I was afraid to run away because I knew he would find me. As I walked home from school with the kids in the neighborhood, I saw someone standing on our porch. Immediately, I am thinking, "Is that him who I'm seeing standing on the porch waiting? What did I do now? If something of his was missing again, I'm sure he misplaced it while he was drunk. But I guess the easiest way out was to blame me. I wished I knew magic. I could make it appear, but he would probably still beat me an yway. To my surprise, he blamed me, but he did not beat me. Instead he punished me. He got on his bicycle and made me get on my little three-wheeler, which was called a Big Wheel. He made me follow him as he rode his bike all over town. My little legs were tired, and I wanted to stop. I was crying, but he made me keep going. When we left the house, it was light outside but, he kept me out until after it was dark. All I wanted to do was just go home.

I think I would rather have received the beating, but little did I know, it was coming later as well. It was a Saturday and my friends GG, Boss Man, Robert Earl [all nicknames and I wouldn't know them today if I saw them] and I were at a store called Piggy Wiggly. We had no money, so we all stole some candy. Of course, we got caught! The store clerk asked, "Do you want me to call your dad or the police?" I remember we threw the candy down and just ran to our houses.

My Joseph Story

From a distance, I could see my house, but I also saw police cars in the yard, about eight of them. I was afraid that they were there to get me for stealing about twenty cents worth of penny candy. I had to think of a lie, but what was I going to say? But when I got there, to my amazement, they weren't there for me! They were there for him; he was fighting my mother.

They arrested him, and he went to jail. Should I have felt bad for feeling happy? But a day later, he was home again. I don't know what happened, because I thought he would be there a long time. After that incident, at least he wasn't beating me like he used to, well not as much.

It was a Sunday afternoon and he was drunk, sitting at the kitchen table asking mom for food. There wasn't enough to go around, but he wanted his and ours.

My mom said, "These kids have got to eat James." As she walked away, he kicked her. A fight broke out and he ran to get his gun. I saw him point the gun at my mom, and I didn't know what to do. Two of my brothers ran into the room and wrestled the gun away from him. Just like that, the nightmare was over. The next day mom put some of us in the car and some of my brothers and sisters on the Greyhound bus and we moved to a new state called Delaware.

It was a long way from home and I was going to miss my friends. We lived with my grandmother and grandfather, who were so nice, in a small town called Millsboro, Delaware.

My first day at my new school and I was in the third grade. I could not believe that I was in a classroom with white kids. It seemed strange, and I could not understand why they could read and write, but I could not. Sadly, I was told it was because I was dumb. I may not have loved going to school, but I loved church. When it was time to go to church, I was all ready to walk into the doors of Holy Trinity Church of God in Christ. The kids liked me there. They didn't talk about me like they did at school. Why was church, Sunday school, and YPWW easier for me than school? I just didn't understand.

I used to help my grandfather take care of his chickens; he had thousands of them. I would help him collect eggs, a lot of eggs!

I could remember everything the preacher preached on the past Sunday, because I would preach it to the chickens. I liked preaching and wanted to be a preacher and a singer when I grew up. I was eight, and I certainly didn't know what prophecy was, but someone said to me, "God is going to make you a preacher."

My pastor told me, "You're a preacher now." I even heard him say, "He's eight years old, but he sounds like a grown man preaching." Well, I couldn't explain it, all I knew was that it made me feel good.

But at that time, all I wanted to know was, would God buy me some Converse sneakers? Everyone had nice shoes except me. I would ask myself, "How do I fix the hole in the bottom of my shoe? I think this cardboard will work. Wow, it does!"

While in grade school, I loved my teacher, but he was mean to me and reminded me of him. I remember one time my teacher asked me, "Do you shower at home?"

"What's that?" I asked. "We wash up by the sink." I guess I didn't wash up well enough. But did he really have to put my desk in the middle of the classroom away from everyone else, and draw a circle with baby powder around my desk, while everyone else teased me and laughed at me? I guess he was teaching me not to come to school smelling bad. How do I make them stop laughing at me? I thought to myself. I know! If I become the class clown, I can make them laugh before they laugh at me, and then I won't know the difference, if they are laughing at me or with me.

At 12 years old, I became a licensed minister. They called me the child evangelist, and I was preaching everywhere. But I still wanted to know if someone could please buy me a pair of shoes? Then one day, one of my teachers, on her lunch break took me downtown to a store called Buster Brown to buy me some sneakers. She said to me, "You can get any pair you want." It was hard for me to decide until I looked on the other side of the store and saw some black patent leather church shoes. I asked, "Can I have those?" "But I thought you wanted sneakers?" she asked.

My honest response was, "I did, but I can see myself in church with these shoes." So, she bought them for me, and I wore them to church and school.

Now I wanted to know if someone could please teach me how to read and write. My grandfather taught me what the preacher said, and I would repeat it after him and memorize it. That was for church, but I still needed help for school. When I was 16, I was placed in a very small classroom of about eight students. They called it "Special Ed." I guess I was a slow learner, but I loved to preach and sing. I wrote a song at 16, but I can't remember the melody. The words said, "I can't let go; no, I won't let go. I'll keep saying it until I see it. I won't stop until I reach it. I can't let go."

Maybe I should put a melody to it now.

At 19-years-old I was an ordained elder and I knew how to read and write! How did it happen? Who finally taught me? God Himself taught me, through giving me the gift of memorization.

When I was 23 years old, Mom had a stroke. She could no longer sing or play the piano and I had to learn to help with everything. While she was in the hospital, I didn't think she was going to make it. How would I live without her? As we funeralized my mother, all I could think of is that she was gone and, what do I do now?

It was 1985, and I was thinking about moving to California and going to Bible college. Was I running from my past or running towards my future? Only time would tell.

Joseph was hated by his brothers, thrown in a pit, left to die, sold into slavery, accused by the wife of the Pharaoh, thrown into prison, and forgotten about by the butler, but was later elevated to the second-in-command in the Pharaoh's kingdom.

In 1991 I wrote my first national hit song, "Press Toward the Mark." Now 55 years later after experiencing such a winding road of experiences, I have gone from the pit to the palace! If you Google or YouTube my name, you will see a visual of the rest of my "Joseph Story".

Psalm 37:23-26

[23] The steps of a good man are ordered by the Lord: and he delighteth in his way.

[24] Though he fall, he shall not be utterly cast down: for the Lord upholdeth him with his hand.

[25] I have been young, and now am old; yet have I not seen the righteous forsaken, nor his seed begging bread.

[26] He is ever merciful, and lendeth; and his seed is blessed.

www.ingramcontent.com/pod-product-compliance
Lightning Source LLC
Chambersburg PA
CBHW070303010526
44108CB00039B/1702